MW01344716

The Christmas Solo Book

24
Arrangements for Medium and High Voice

Compiled by *Tom Fettke*

KANSAS CITY, MO 64141

Copyright © 2001 Pilot Point Music • All rights reserved. • Litho in U.S.A.
www.lillenas.com

Contents

A Cradle in the Shadow of a Cross 32
Alleluia, Christ Is Born *with* What Child Is This? 68
Arise! Shine! 88
GO TELL IT! 39
    The Virgin Mary Had a Baby Boy
    Go, Tell It on the Mountain
Heaven's Child 63
I Cannot Tell 94
I Will Rejoice 26
In the First Light 152
Jesus, the Light of the World 55
LET US ADORE HIM 115
    Gesu Bambino
    Jesus
My Eyes Have Seen Your Salvation 132
O Come, O Come, Emmanuel 45
O Holy Night 121
O Lord, Most Holy 75
One Life 103
One Quiet Moment 125
Precious Promise 12
Rose of Bethlehem 5
STAR OF WONDER 108
    We Three Kings
    Beautiful Star of Bethlehem
The Birthday of a King 82
There Is Hope 146
Thou Didst Leave Thy Throne 20
What's Christmas Without Jesus? 50
Who Is This Child? 139

Rose of Bethlehem

Words and Music by
LOWELL ALEXANDER
Arranged by Richard Kingsmore

© 1992 Birdwing Music (ASCAP). Admin. by EMI Christian Music Publishing.
All rights reserved. Used by permission.

PLEASE NOTE: Copying of this product is not covered by CCLI licenses. For CCLI information call 1-800-234-2446.

Precious Promise

Words and Music by
STEVEN CURTIS CHAPMAN
Arranged by Tom Fettke

Gently ♩ = ca. 108

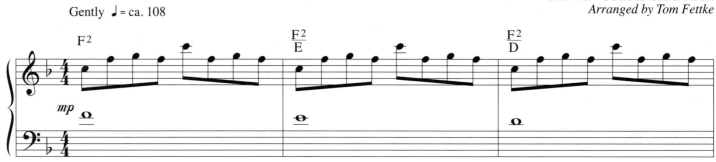

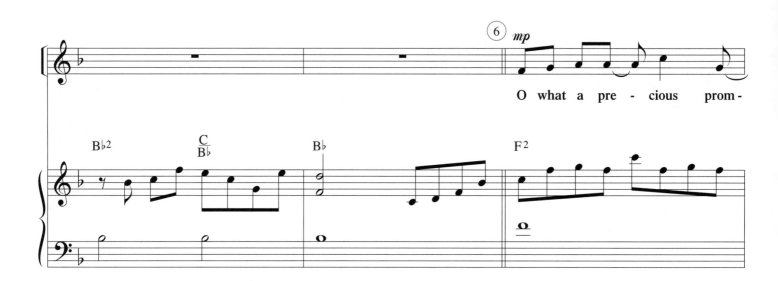

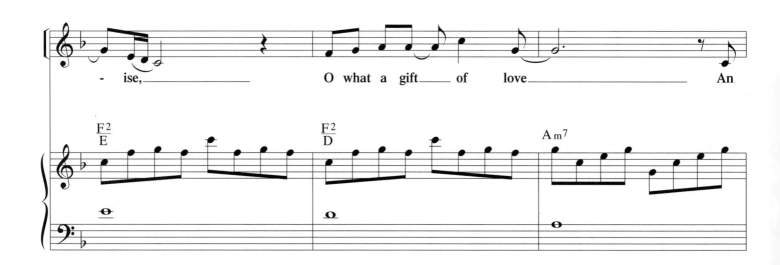

© 1995 Sparrow Song (BMI) and Peach Hill Songs (BMI). Admin. by
EMI Christian Music Publishing. All rights reserved. Used by permission.

PLEASE NOTE: Copying of this product is not covered by CCLI licenses. For CCLI information call 1-800-234-2446.

Thou Didst Leave Thy Throne

EMILY E. S. ELLIOTT

TIMOTHY R. MATTHEWS
Arranged by Richard Kingsmore

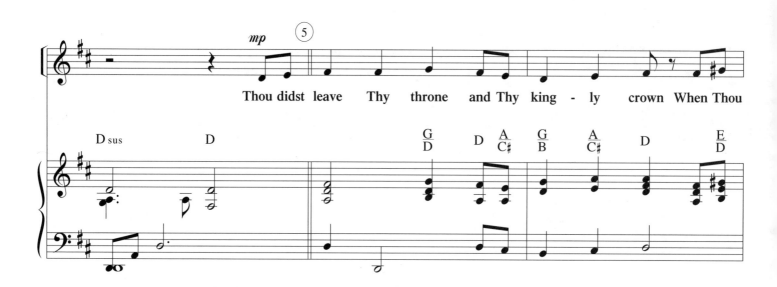

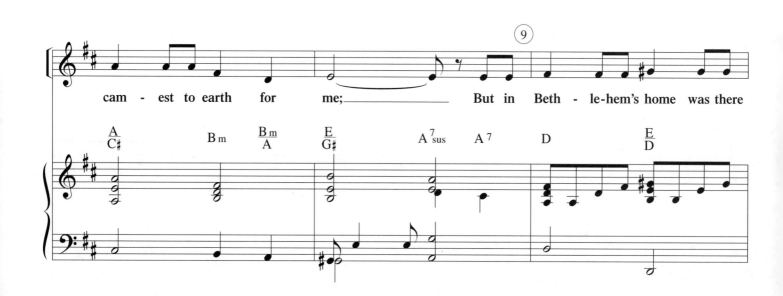

Arr. © 2000 by Pilot Point Music (ASCAP). All rights reserved.
Administered by The Copyright Company, 40 Music Square East, Nashville, TN 37203.

PLEASE NOTE: Copying of this product is not covered by CCLI licenses. For CCLI information call 1-800-234-2446.

*The original text is "My heart shall rejoice, Lord Jesus, when Thou comest and callest for me." This piece may be used as an invitation, so the text included in the music is more appropriate.

I Will Rejoice

Luke 1
Adapted by KEITH FERGUSON

BRUCE GREER
Arranged by Bruce Greer

Copyright © 1996 by Pilot Point Music (ASCAP). All rights reserved.
Administered by The Copyright Company, 40 Music Square East, Nashville, TN 37203.

PLEASE NOTE: Copying of this product is not covered by CCLI licenses. For CCLI information call 1-800-234-2446.

A Cradle in the Shadow of a Cross

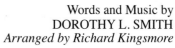

*Words by JOHN W. WORK, JR.; Music, Spiritual. Arr. © 1998 by Pilot Point Music (ASCAP). All rights reserved. Administered by The Copyright Company, 40 Music Square East, Nashville, TN 37203.

O Come, O Come, Emmanuel

Latin Hymn;
Tr. by JOHN M. NEALE

STEVEN CURTIS CHAPMAN
Arranged by Tom Fettke

© 1995 Sparrow Song (BMI) and Peach Hill Songs (BMI) (both admin. by
EMI Christian Music Publishing). All rights reserved. Used by permission.

PLEASE NOTE: Copying of this product is not covered by CCLI licenses. For CCLI information call 1-800-234-2446.

What's Christmas Without Jesus?

NAN ALLEN

DENNIS ALLEN
Arranged by Dennis Allen

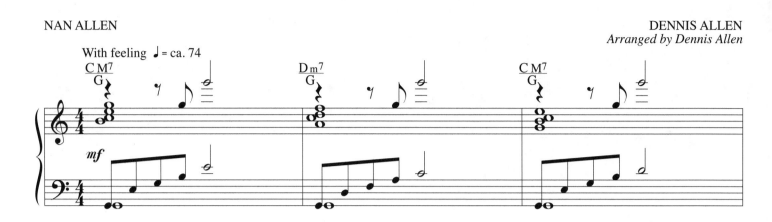

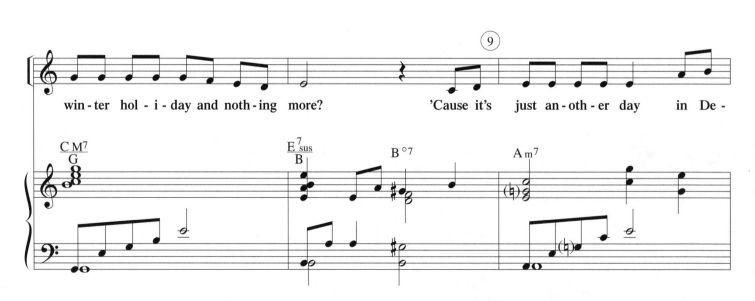

Copyright © 1988, and this arr. © 1999 by Pilot Point Music (ASCAP). All rights reserved.
Administered by The Copyright Company, 40 Music Square East, Nashville, TN 37203.

PLEASE NOTE: Copying of this product is not covered by CCLI licenses. For CCLI information call 1-800-234-2446.

Jesus, the Light of the World

CHARLES WESLEY and
GEORGE D. ELDERKIN

GEORGE D. ELDERKIN
Arranged by Tom Fettke

Arr. © 1998 by Pilot Point Music (ASCAP). All rights reserved.
Administered by The Copyright Company, 40 Music Square East, Nashville, TN 37203.

PLEASE NOTE: Copying of this product is not covered by CCLI licenses. For CCLI information call 1-800-234-2446.

Alleluia, Christ Is Born

with
What Child Is This?

Words and Music by
TWILA PARIS
Arranged by Joseph Linn

© 1989 Ariose Music/Mountain Spring Music (ASCAP)
Admin. by EMI Christian Music Publishing. All rights reserved. Used by permission.

PLEASE NOTE: Copying of this product is not covered by CCLI licenses. For CCLI information call 1-800-234-2446.

O Lord, Most Holy

KEN BIBLE

CÉSAR FRANCK
Arranged by Tom Fettke

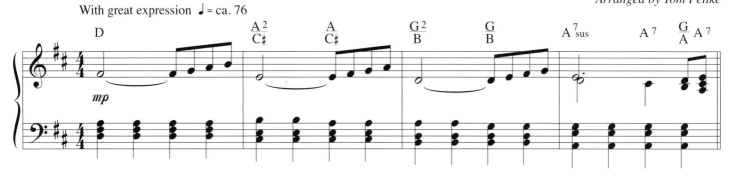
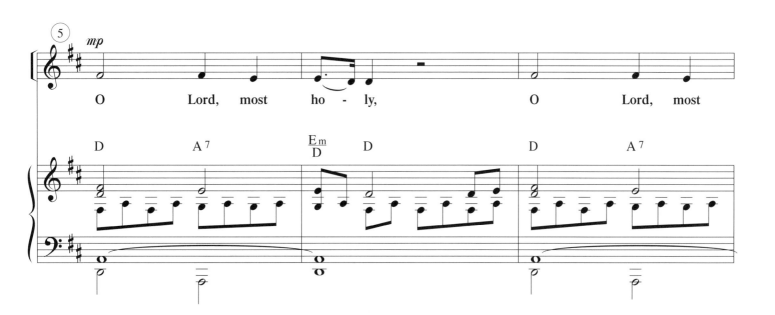
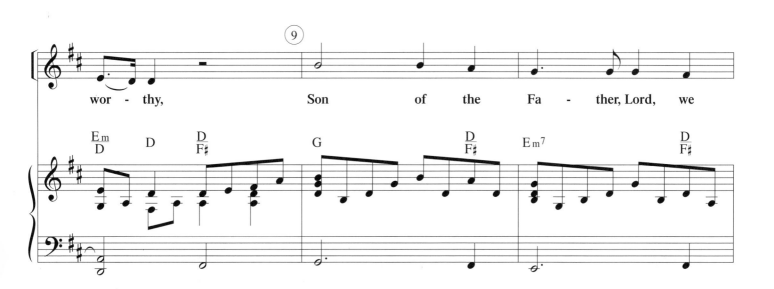

Copyright © 1999 by Pilot Point Music (ASCAP). All rights reserved.
Administered by The Copyright Company, 40 Music Square East, Nashville, TN 37203.

PLEASE NOTE: Copying of this product is not covered by CCLI licenses. For CCLI information call 1-800-234-2446.

The Birthday of a King

Words and Music by
W. H. NEIDLINGER
Arranged by Tom Fettke

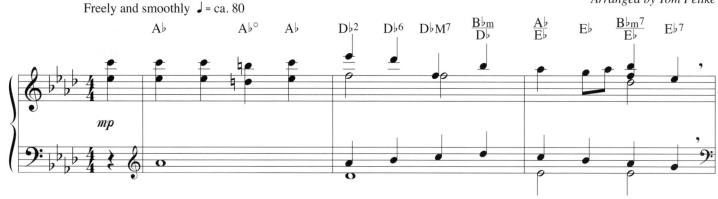
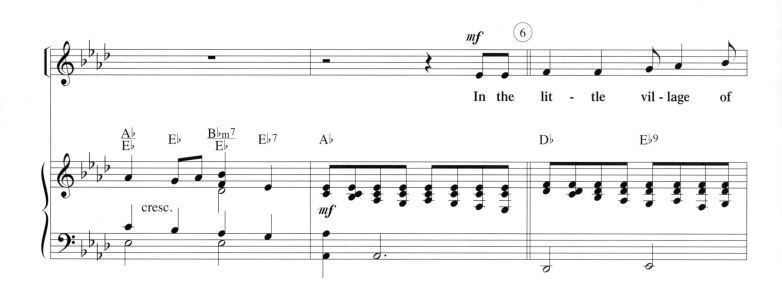
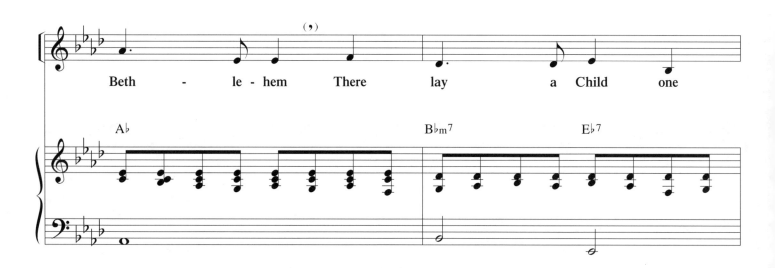

Arr. © 1985, 1995 by Pilot Point Music (ASCAP). All rights reserved.
Administered by The Copyright Company, 40 Music Square East, Nashville, TN 37203.

PLEASE NOTE: Copying of this product is not covered by CCLI licenses. For CCLI information call 1-800-234-2446.

Star of Wonder

We Three Kings
Beautiful Star of Bethlehem

Arranged by Tom Fettke

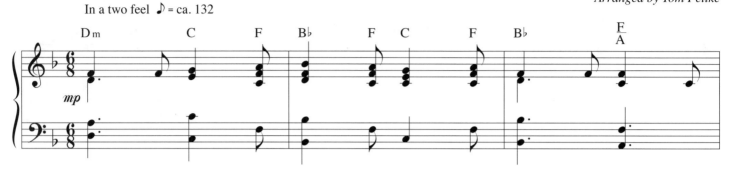
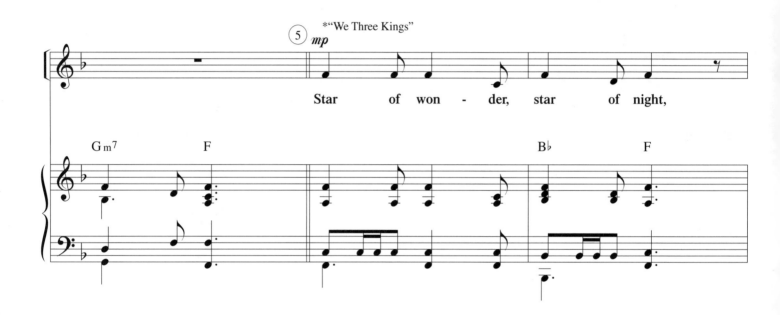

*Words and Music by JOHN H. HOPKINS, JR. Arr. © 1998 by Pilot Point Music (ASCAP). All rights reserved. Administered by The Copyright Company, 40 Music Square East, Nashville, TN 37203.

PLEASE NOTE: Copying of this product is not covered by CCLI licenses. For CCLI information call 1-800-234-2446.

*"Beautiful Star of Bethlehem"

*Words by ADGER M. PACE; Music by R. FISCHER BOYCE. © 1940 (Renewal 1967) James D. Vaughan Music Publisher/SESAC (a div. of SpiritSound Music Group). All rights reserved. Used by permission.

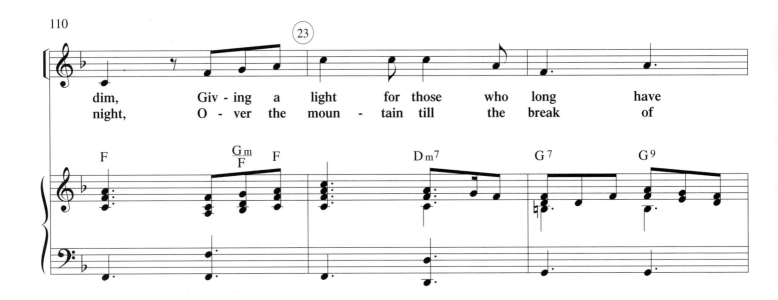

Let Us Adore Him

Gesu Bambino
Jesus

Arranged by Tom Fettke

Gently ♩. = ca. 58

1. When
(2. Our)

*"Gesu Bambino"

1. blos-soms flow-ered mid the snows, Up-on a win-ter night Was
2. God so pure, so high a-bove, Is pleased to come and dwell. Come

1. born the Child, the Christ-mas Rose, The King of Love and Light. The
2. see the mys-t'ry of His love: A Child, Em-man-u-el. The

*Words by FREDERICK H. MARTENS and KEN BIBLE; Music by PIETRO A. YON. Copyright © 1998 by Pilot Point Music (ASCAP). All rights reserved. Administered by The Copyright Company, 40 Music Square East, Nashville, TN 37203.

PLEASE NOTE: Copying of this product is not covered by CCLI licenses. For CCLI information call 1-800-234-2446.

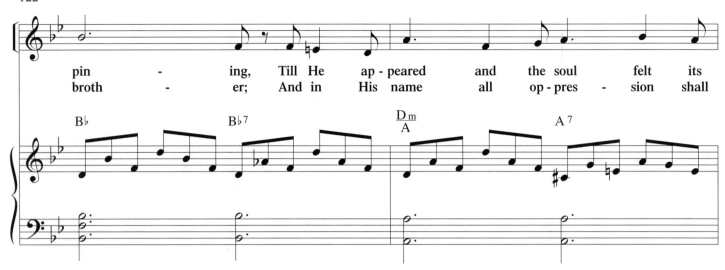
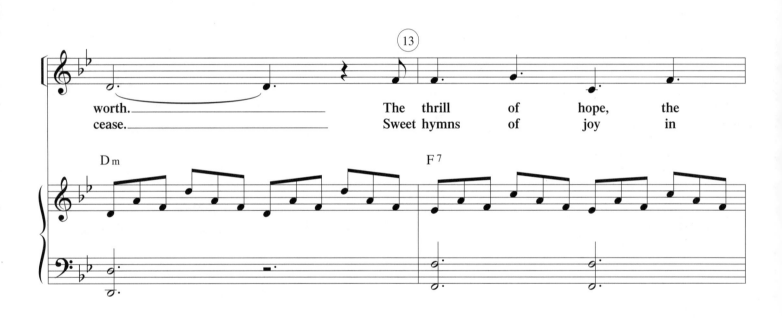

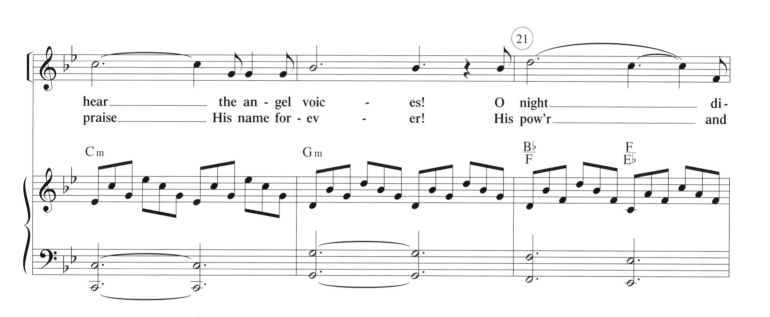

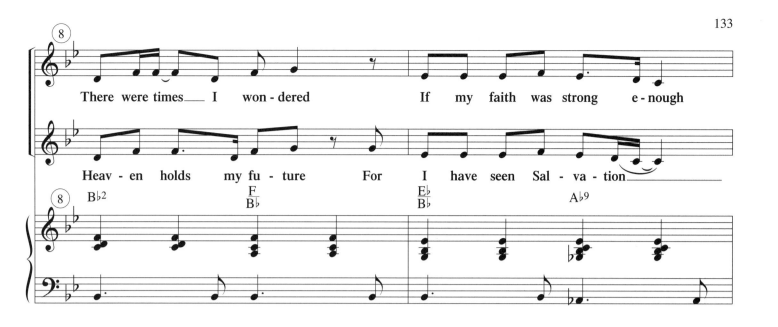
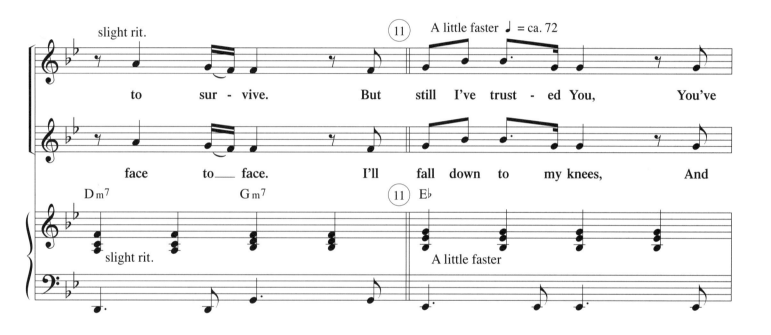
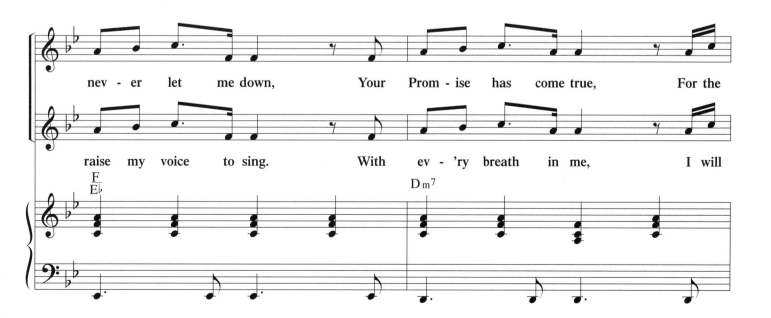

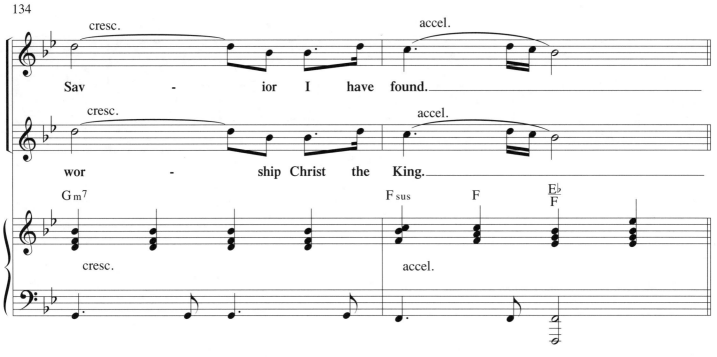

Who Is This Child?

PATRICIA KING STOWELL

BENJAMIN HARLAN
Arranged by Tom Fettke

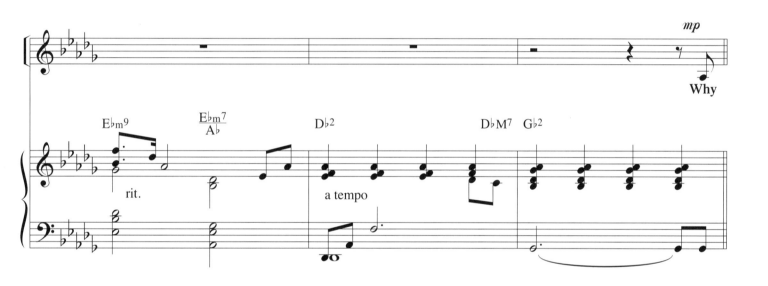

Copyright © 1990, and this arr. © 2000 by Pilot Point Music (ASCAP). All rights reserved.
Administered by The Copyright Company, 40 Music Square East, Nashville, TN 37203.

PLEASE NOTE: Copying of this product is not covered by CCLI licenses. For CCLI information call 1-800-234-2446.

In the First Light

Words and Music by
BOB KAUFLIN
Arranged by Tom Fettke

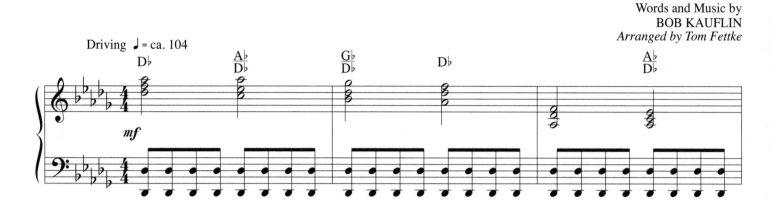
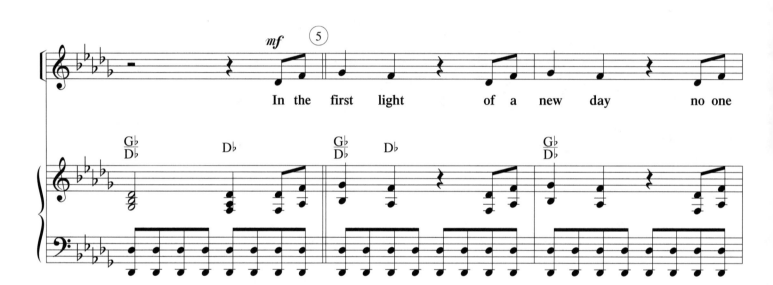
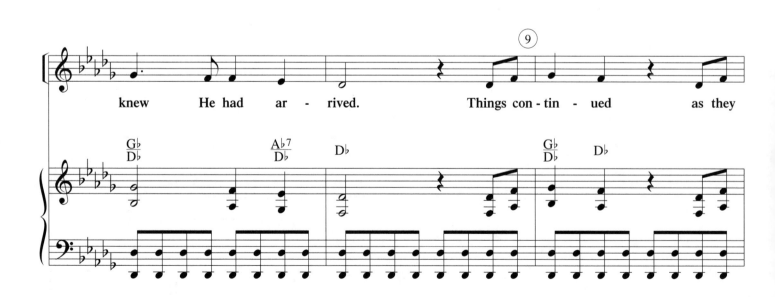

© Copyright 1988 LifeSong Music Press. (Admin. by Brentwood-Benson Music Publishing). All rights reserved. Used by permission.

PLEASE NOTE: Copying of this product is not covered by CCLI licenses. For CCLI information call 1-800-234-2446.